A Day of Play

With LeVon, Langston, and Faith!

Summer Vacation

Concept By: LaTonya Jones

Illustrated By: Mehk Arshad

Written By: Latonya Jones Langston and

LaToya Stafford Brittany Smalls

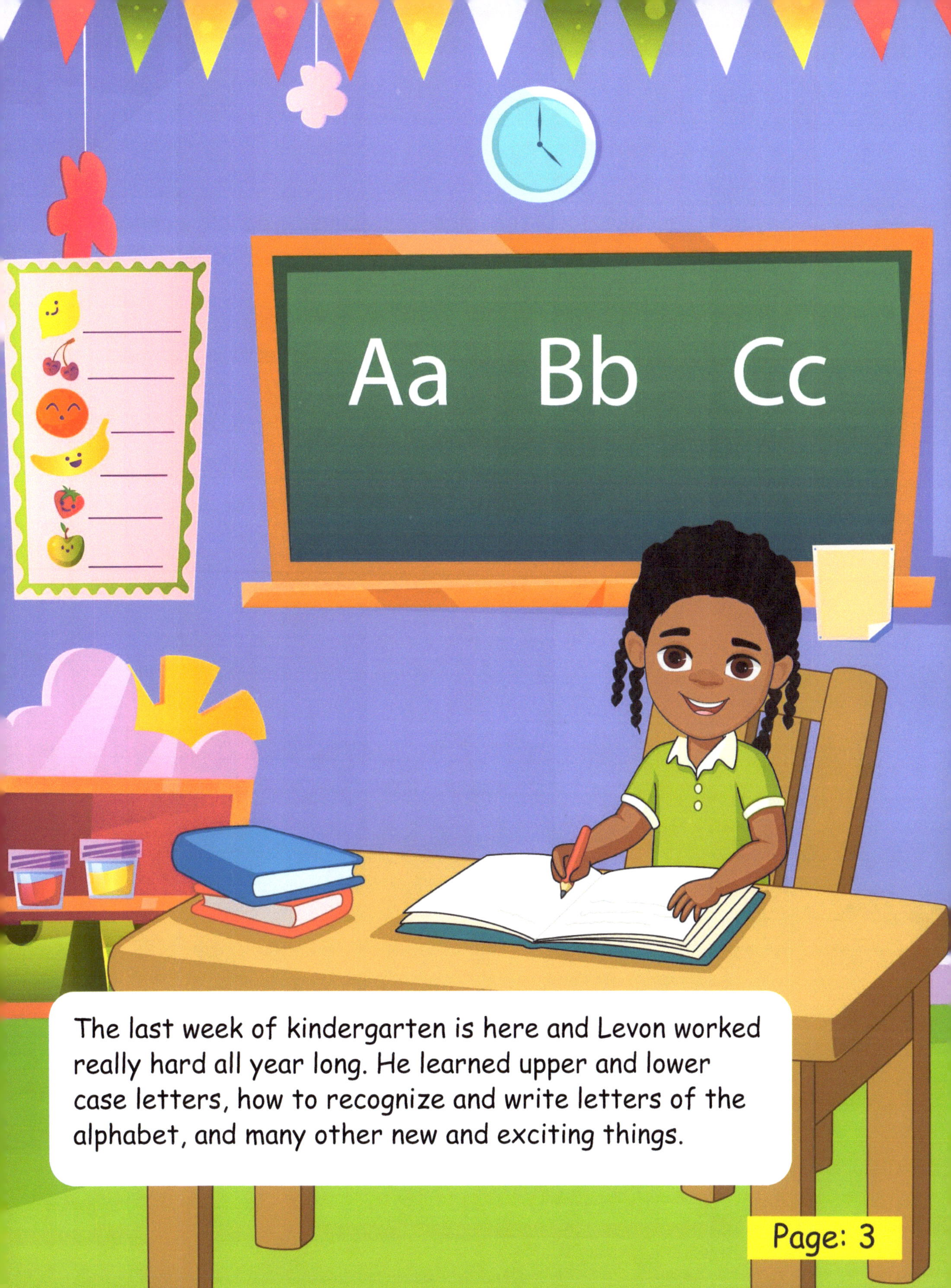

The last week of kindergarten is here and Levon worked really hard all year long. He learned upper and lower case letters, how to recognize and write letters of the alphabet, and many other new and exciting things.

Levon's teacher told the class, "Because you all worked really, really hard this school year, how about we put on a performance to celebrate your accomplishments?"

The children were overjoyed with this news as they jumped for joy.

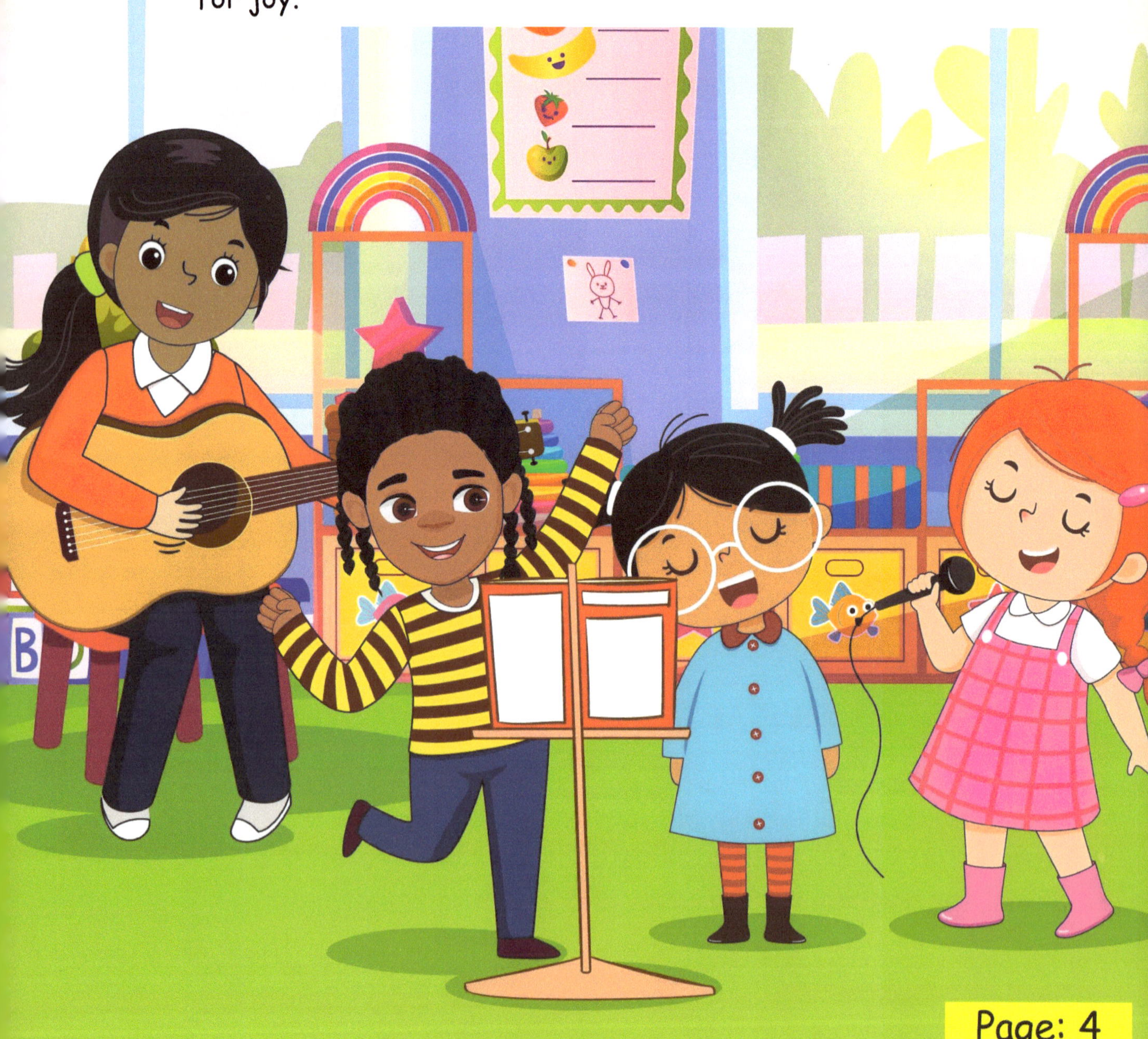

After many days of long, hard practicing, the day of the performance was finally here. As Levon was getting ready for school, he thought to himself, "I can't wait to show everyone what we've been working on!"

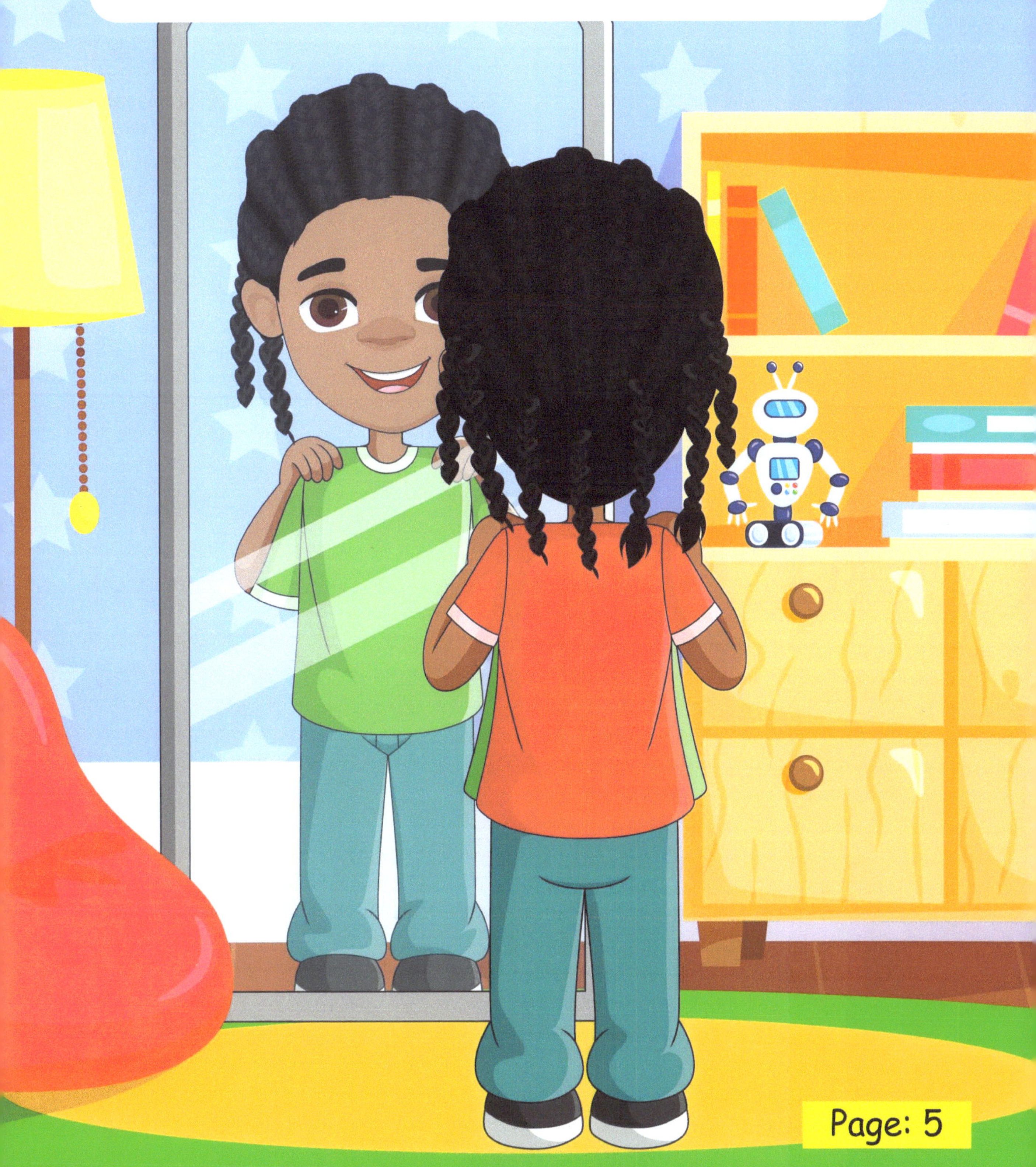

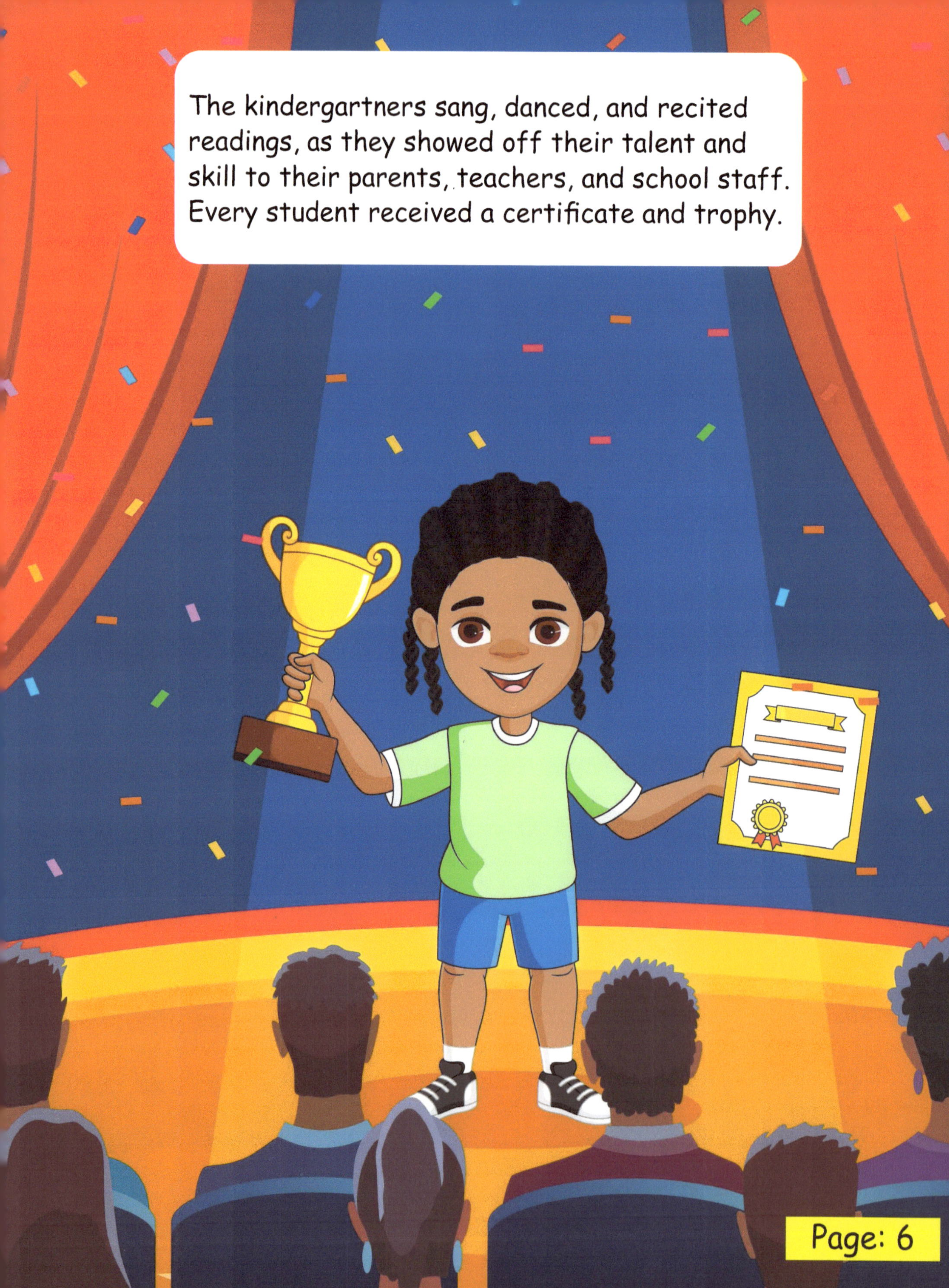
The kindergartners sang, danced, and recited readings, as they showed off their talent and skill to their parents, teachers, and school staff. Every student received a certificate and trophy.

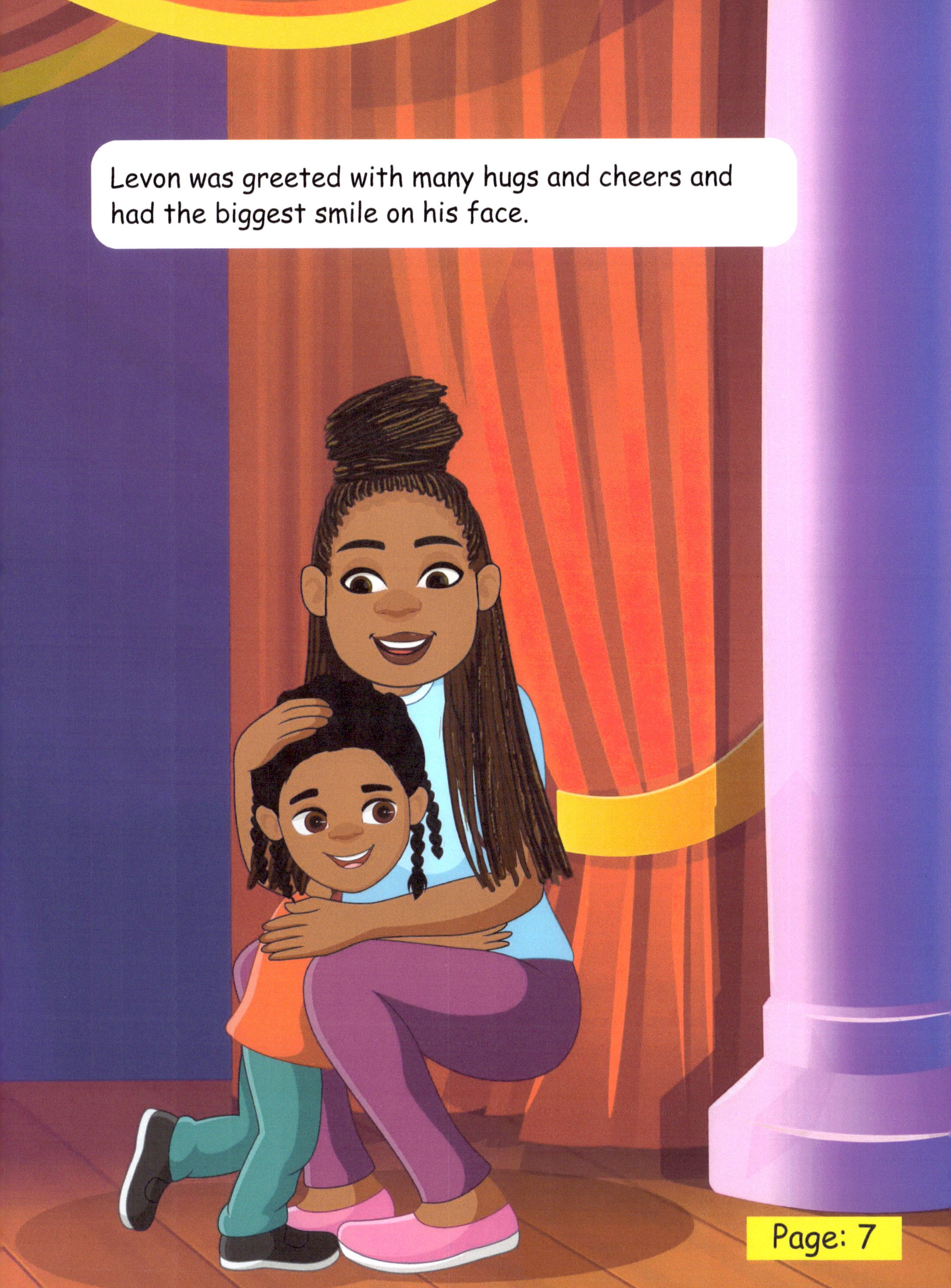
Levon was greeted with many hugs and cheers and had the biggest smile on his face.

Back at home, Levon's cousins, Langston and Faith came over to continue the celebration. Langston and Faith also graduated from kindergarten too! To reward them for their hard work, the parents decided to take the cousins on a summer vacation.

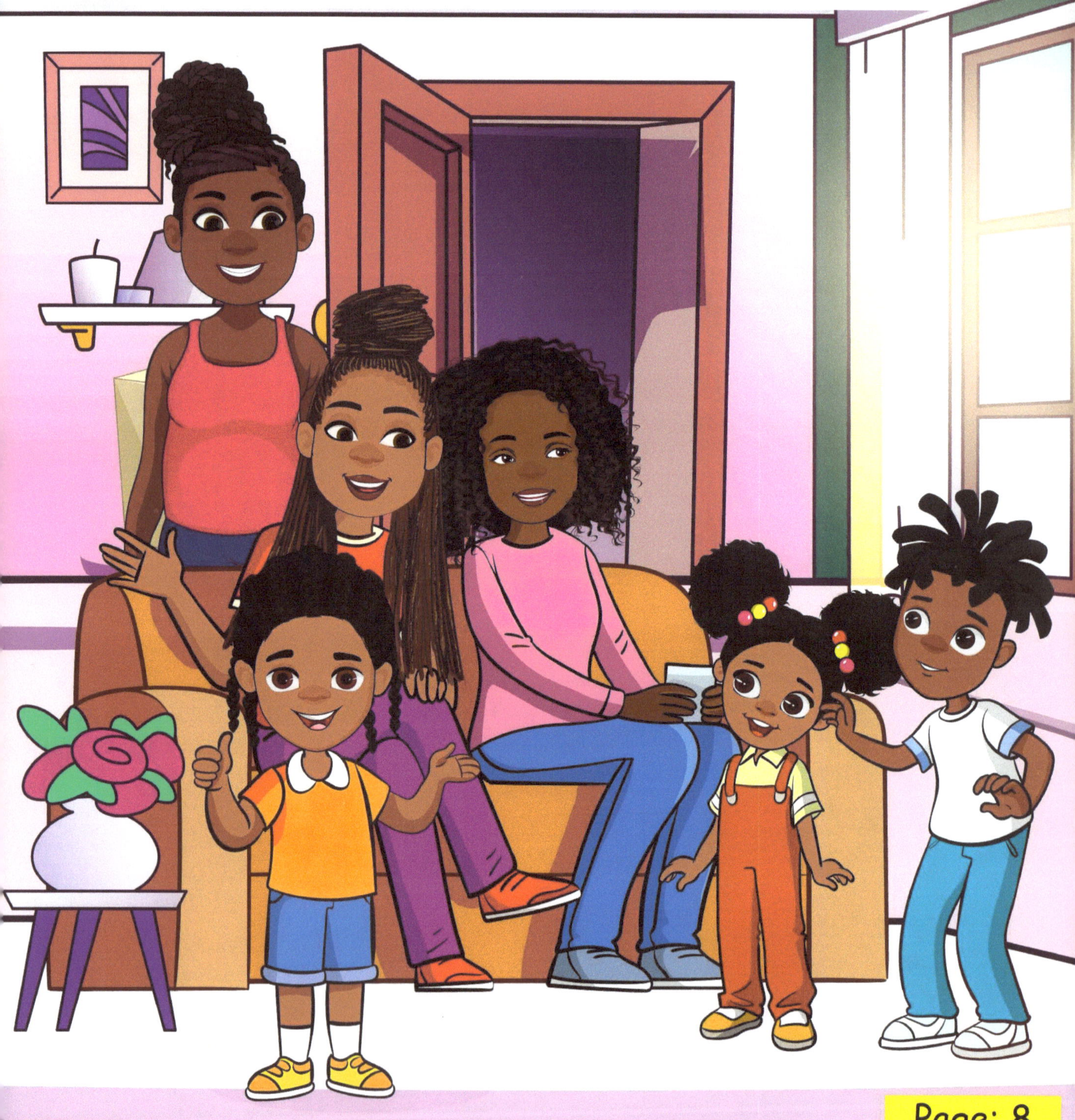

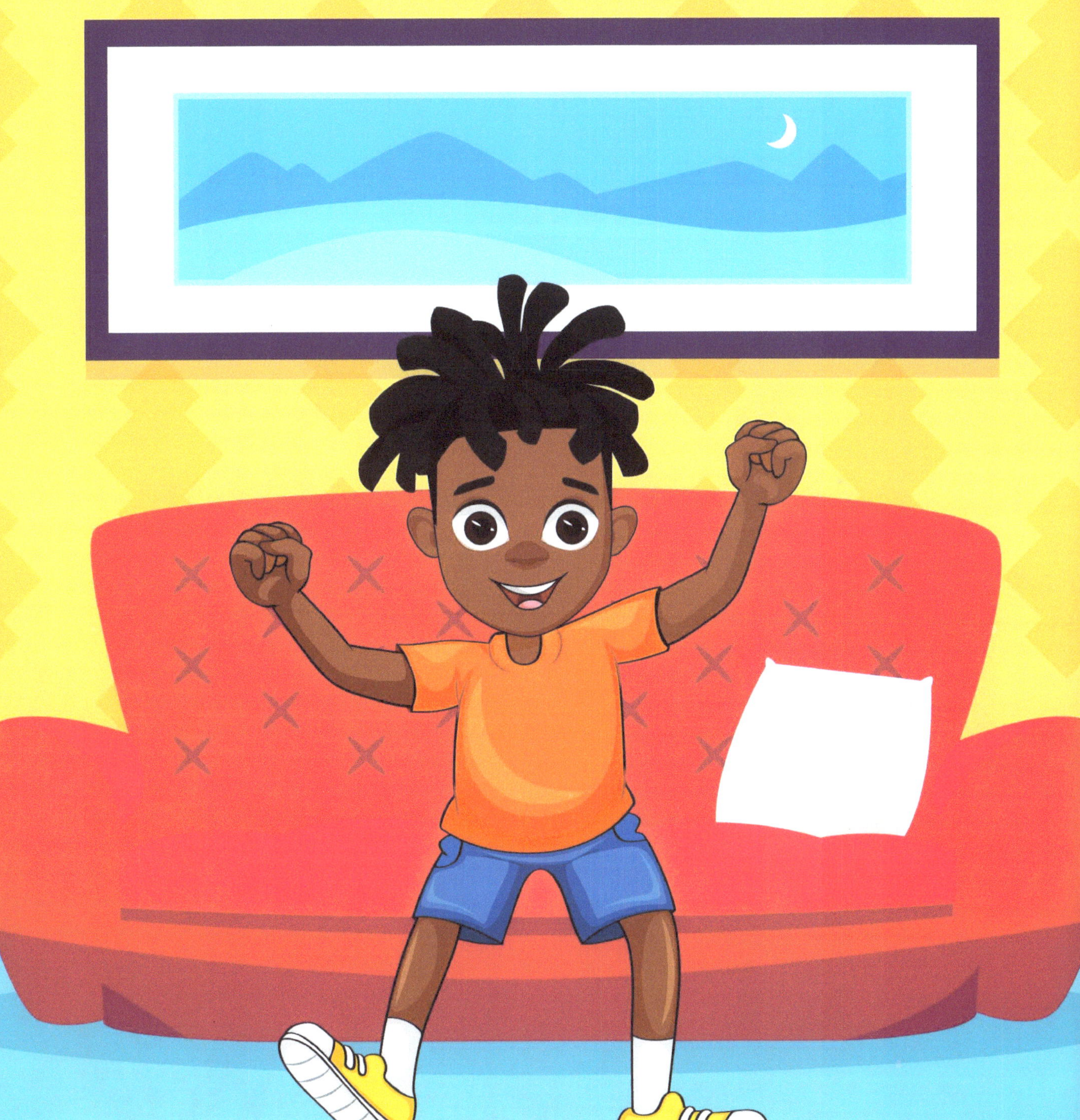

Langston was surprised to learn about the summer vacation. In addition to spending time with his favorite cousins, he enjoyed visiting different cities, learning about different cultures, and meeting new people.

To prepare for the vacation, Langston and his mom created a list of things he would need to bring.

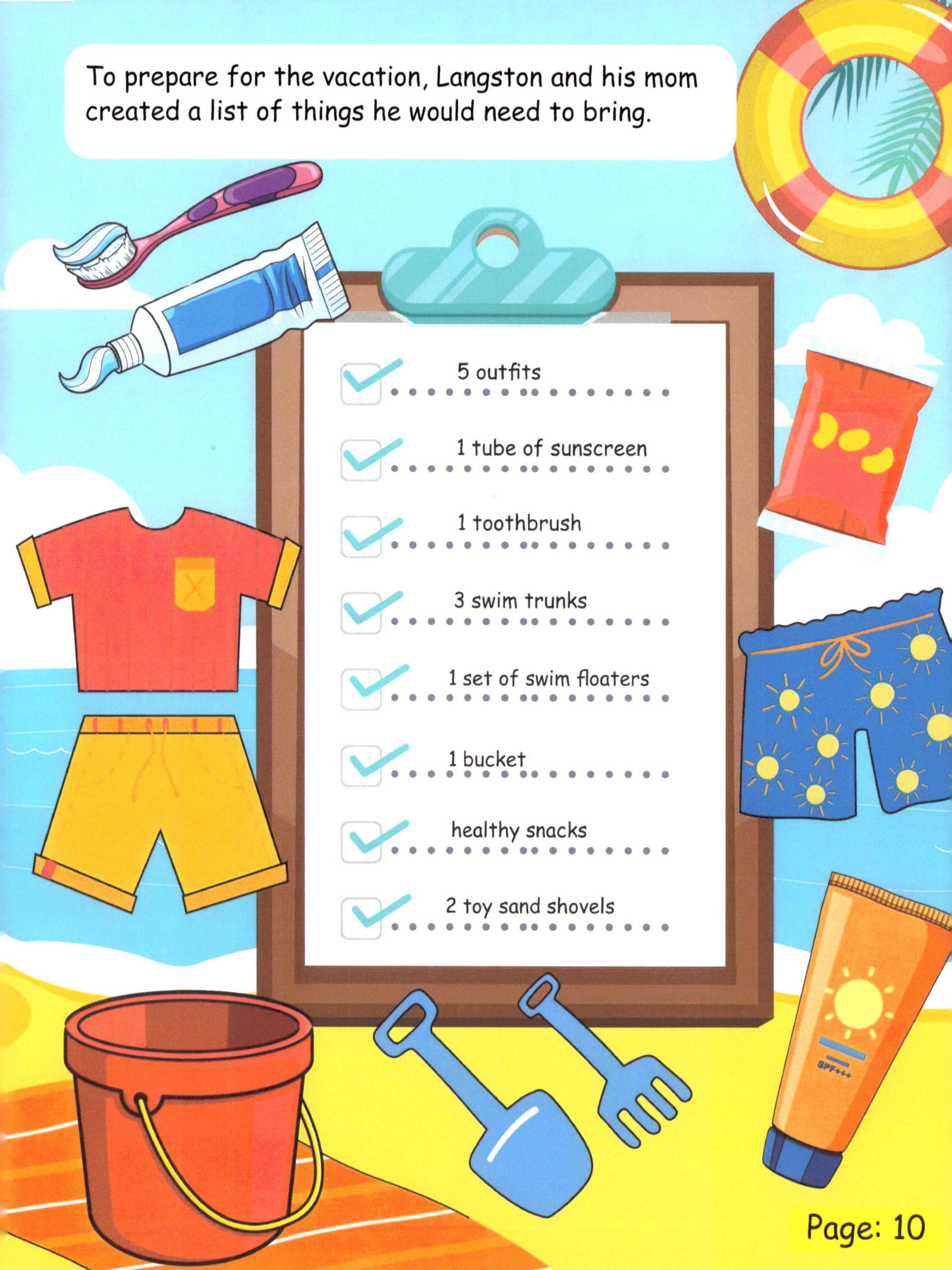

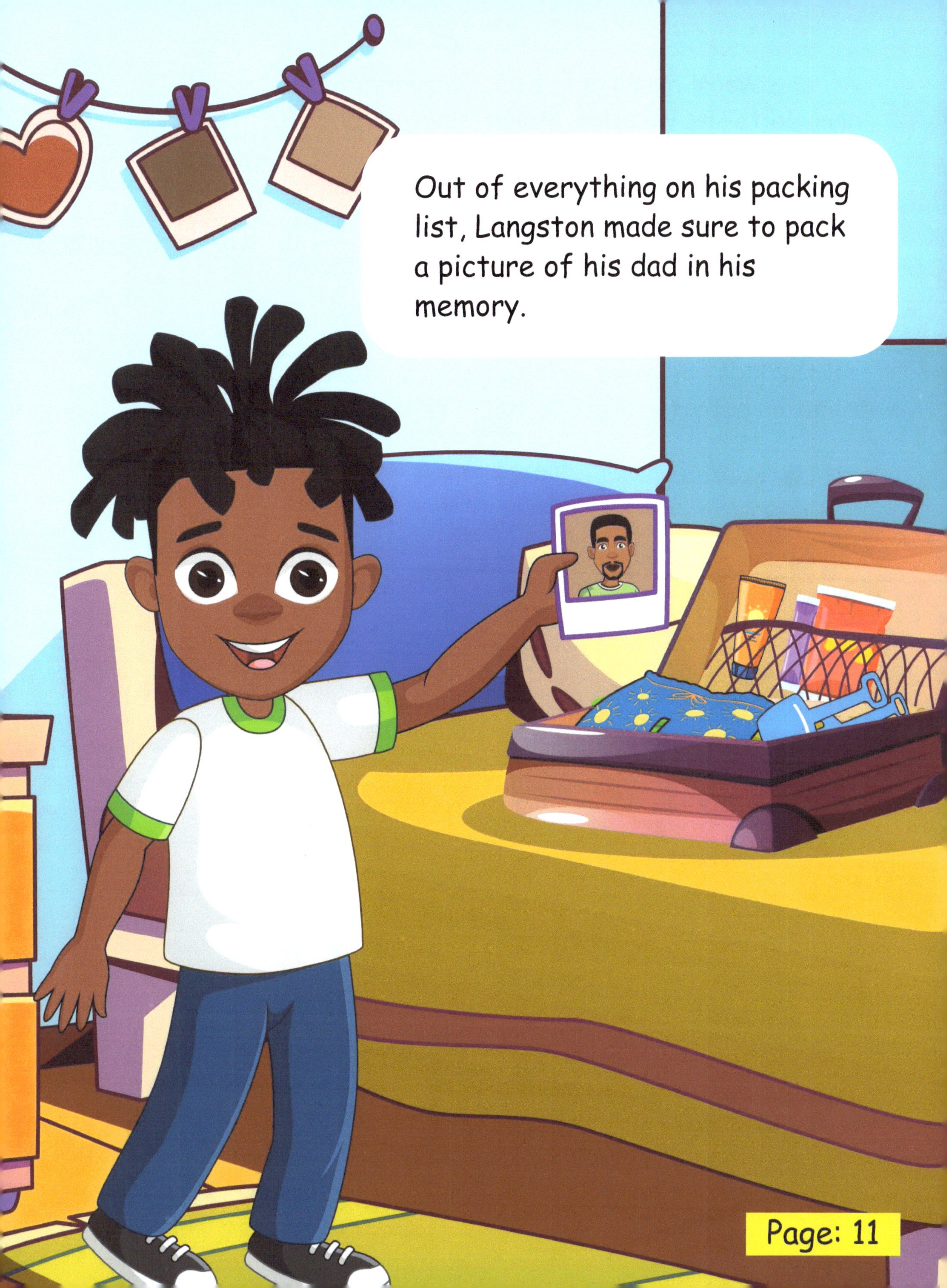
Out of everything on his packing list, Langston made sure to pack a picture of his dad in his memory.

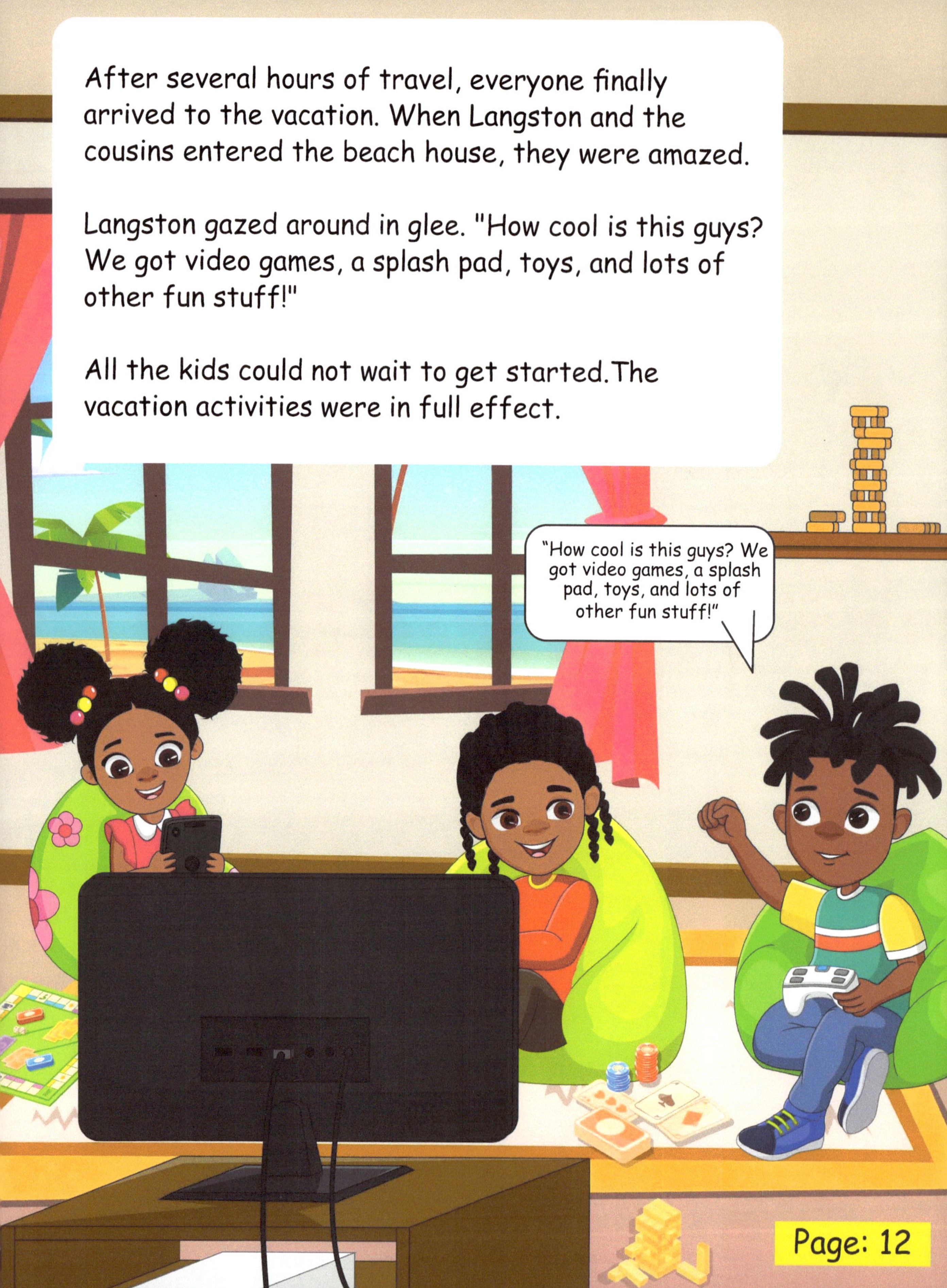
After several hours of travel, everyone finally arrived to the vacation. When Langston and the cousins entered the beach house, they were amazed.
Langston gazed around in glee. "How cool is this guys? We got video games, a splash pad, toys, and lots of other fun stuff!"
All the kids could not wait to get started.The vacation activities were in full effect.
"How cool is this guys? We got video games, a splash pad, toys, and lots of other fun stuff!"

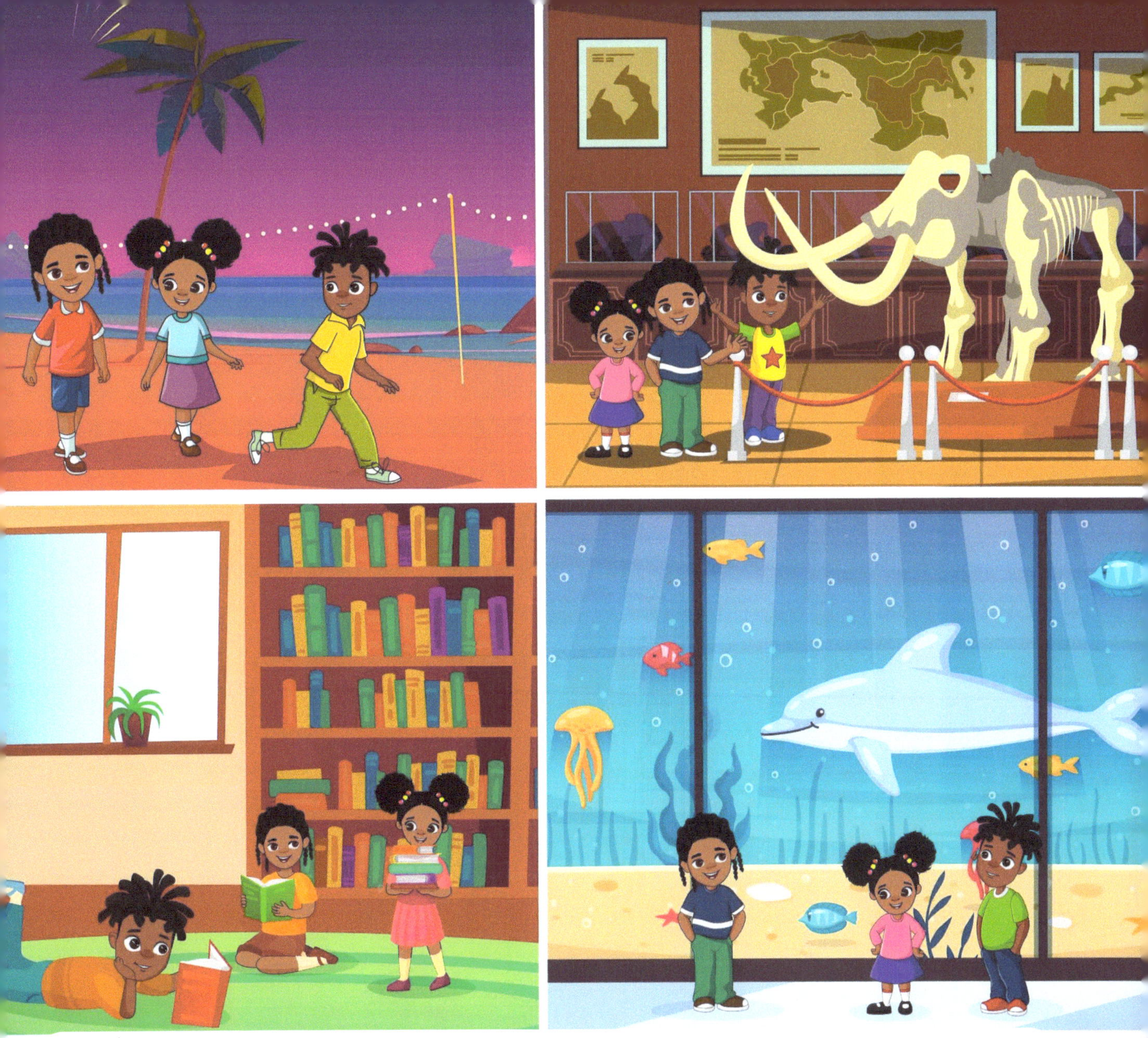

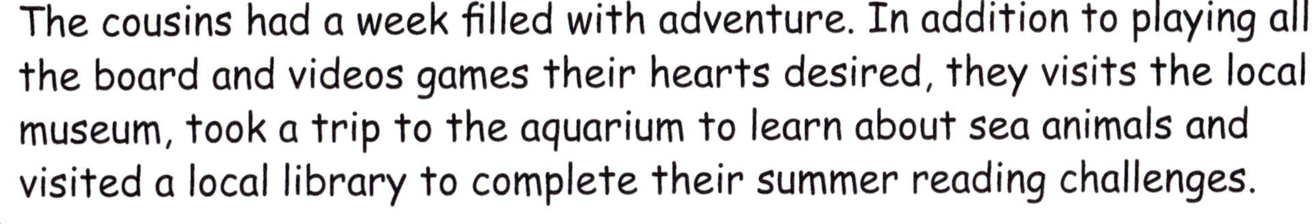

The cousins had a week filled with adventure. In addition to playing all the board and videos games their hearts desired, they visits the local museum, took a trip to the aquarium to learn about sea animals and visited a local library to complete their summer reading challenges.

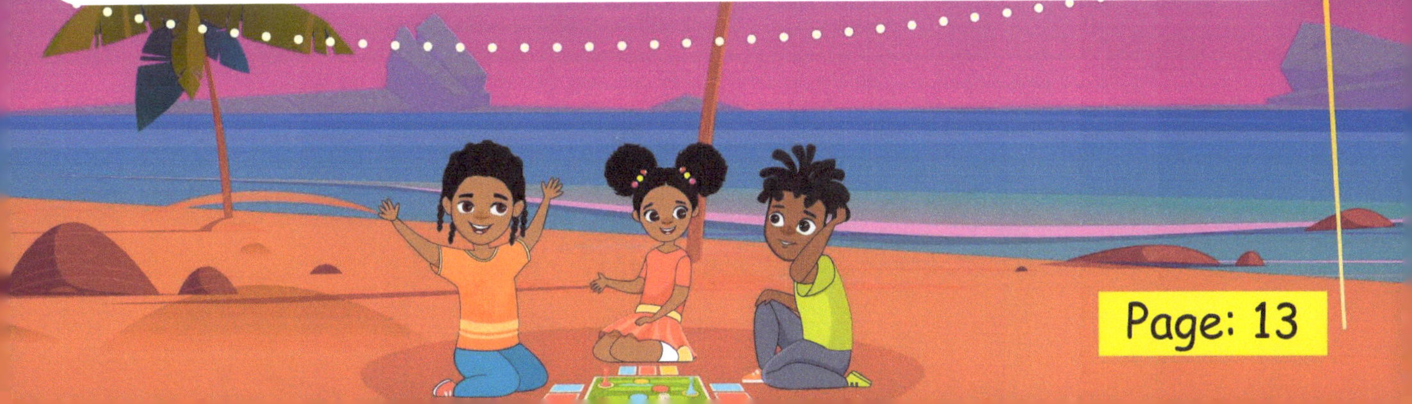

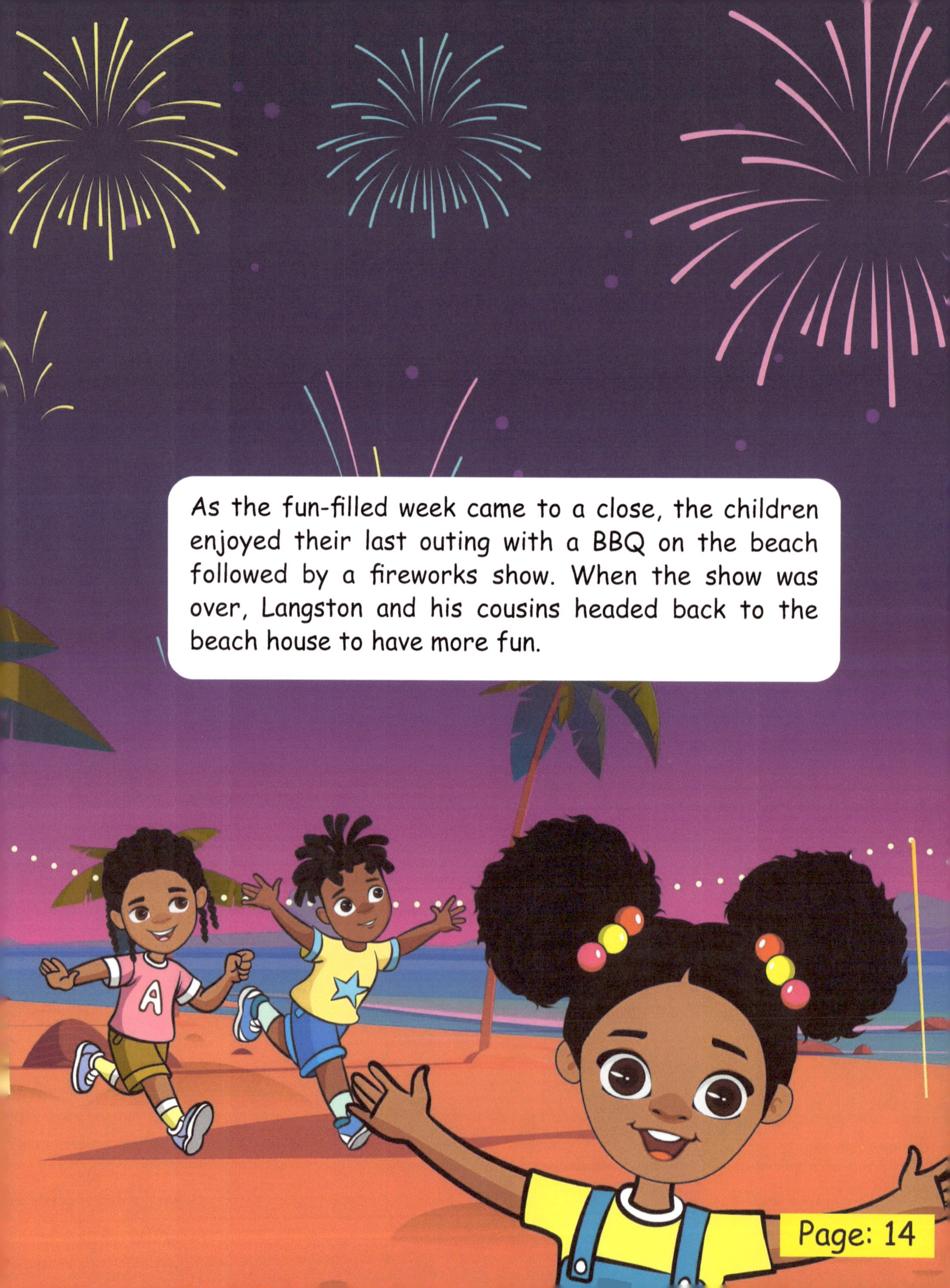

As the fun-filled week came to a close, the children enjoyed their last outing with a BBQ on the beach followed by a fireworks show. When the show was over, Langston and his cousins headed back to the beach house to have more fun.

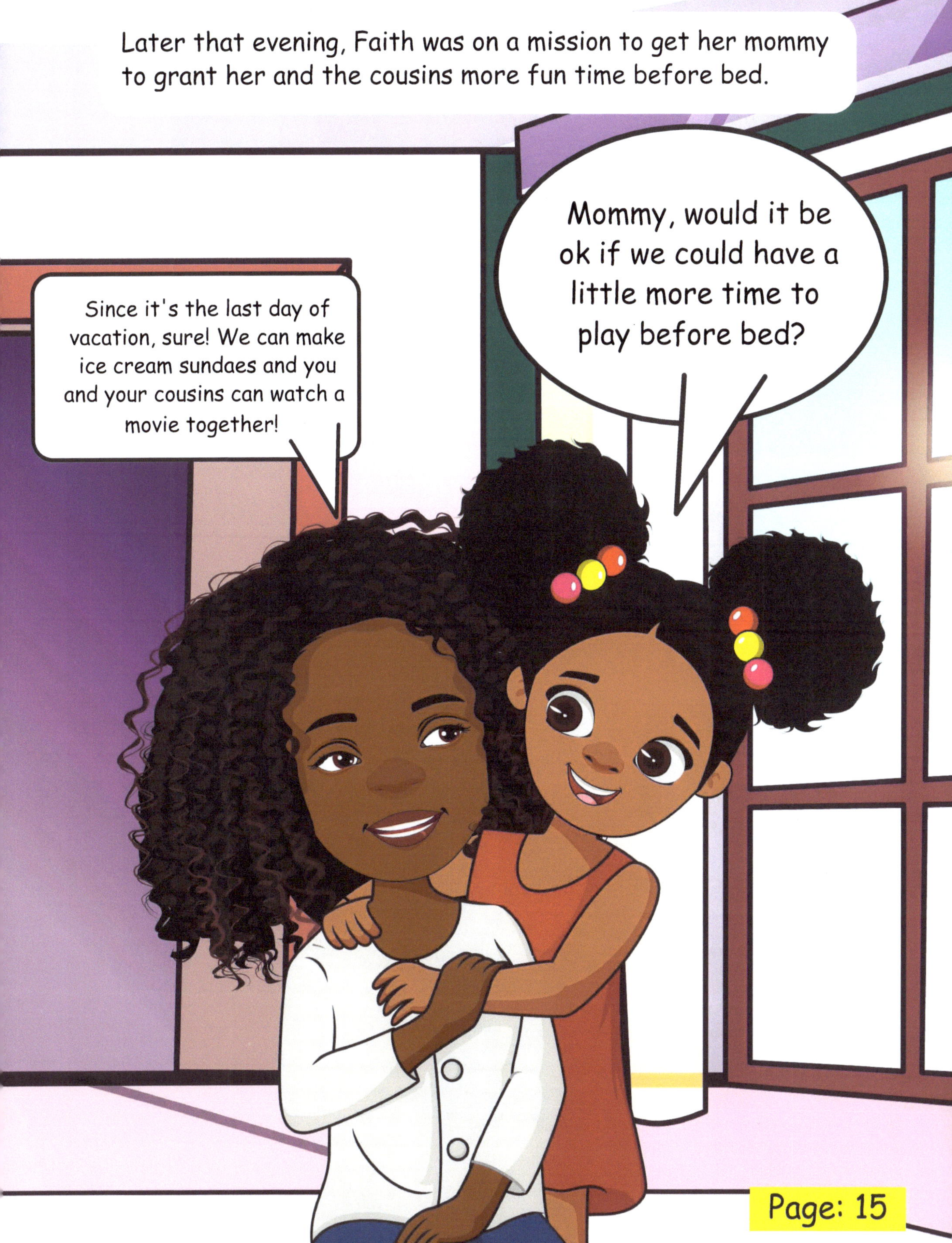
Later that evening, Faith was on a mission to get her mommy to grant her and the cousins more fun time before bed.
Mommy, would it be ok if we could have a little more time to play before bed?
Since it's the last day of vacation, sure! We can make ice cream sundaes and you and your cousins can watch a movie together!

"Yay!" Shouted Faith as she ran to the room to tell Levon and Langston the good news.

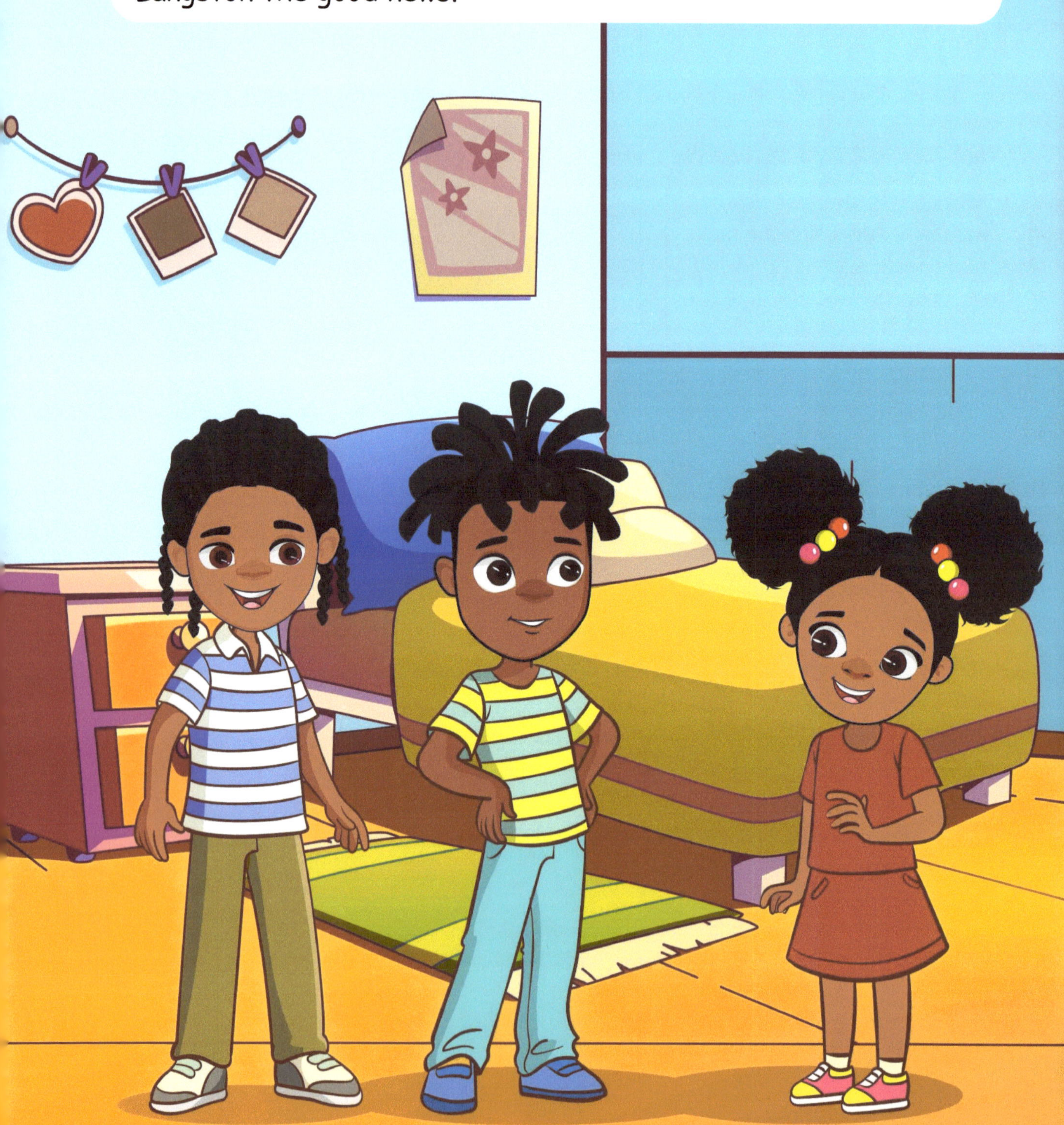

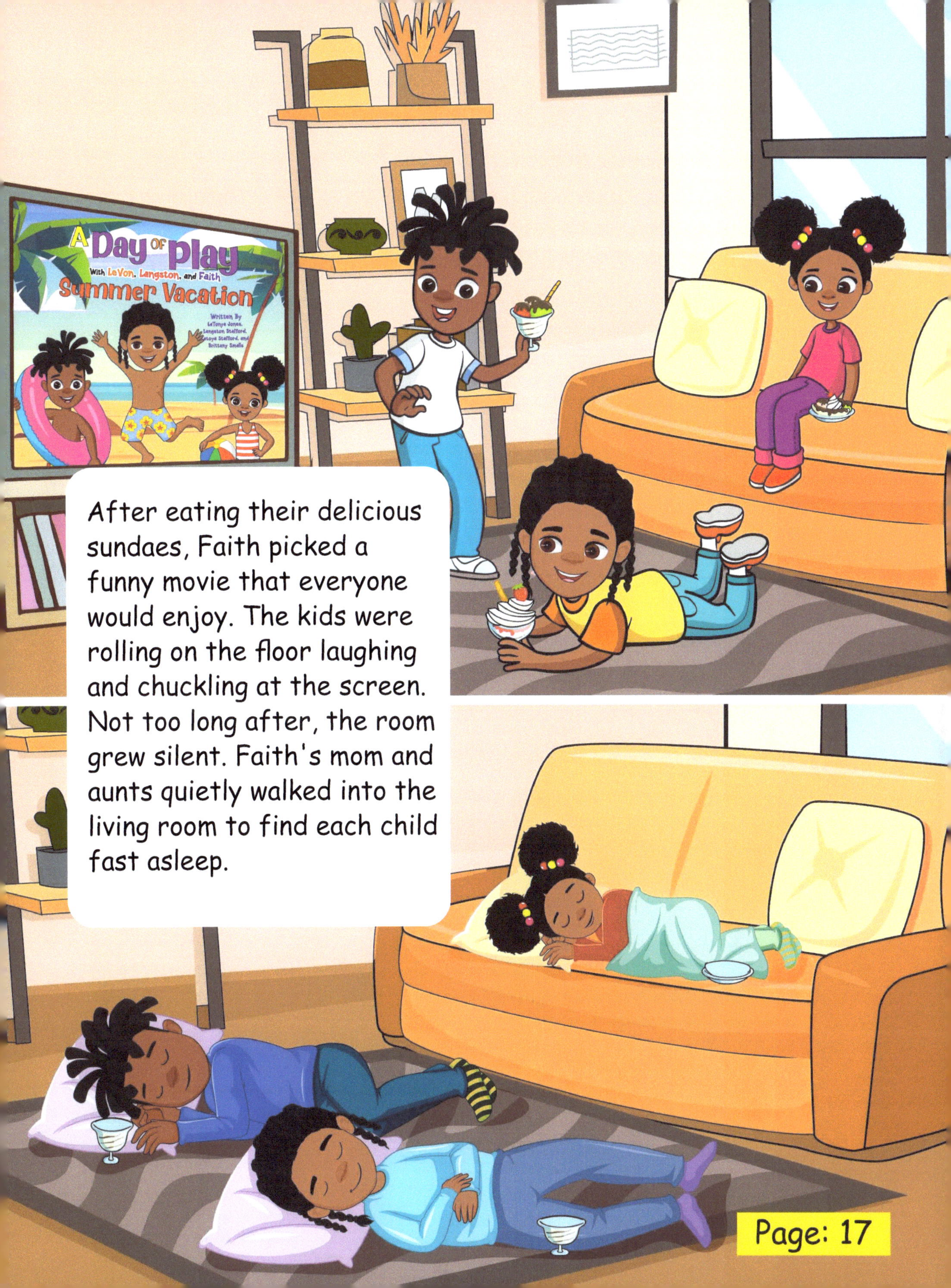

After eating their delicious sundaes, Faith picked a funny movie that everyone would enjoy. The kids were rolling on the floor laughing and chuckling at the screen. Not too long after, the room grew silent. Faith's mom and aunts quietly walked into the living room to find each child fast asleep.

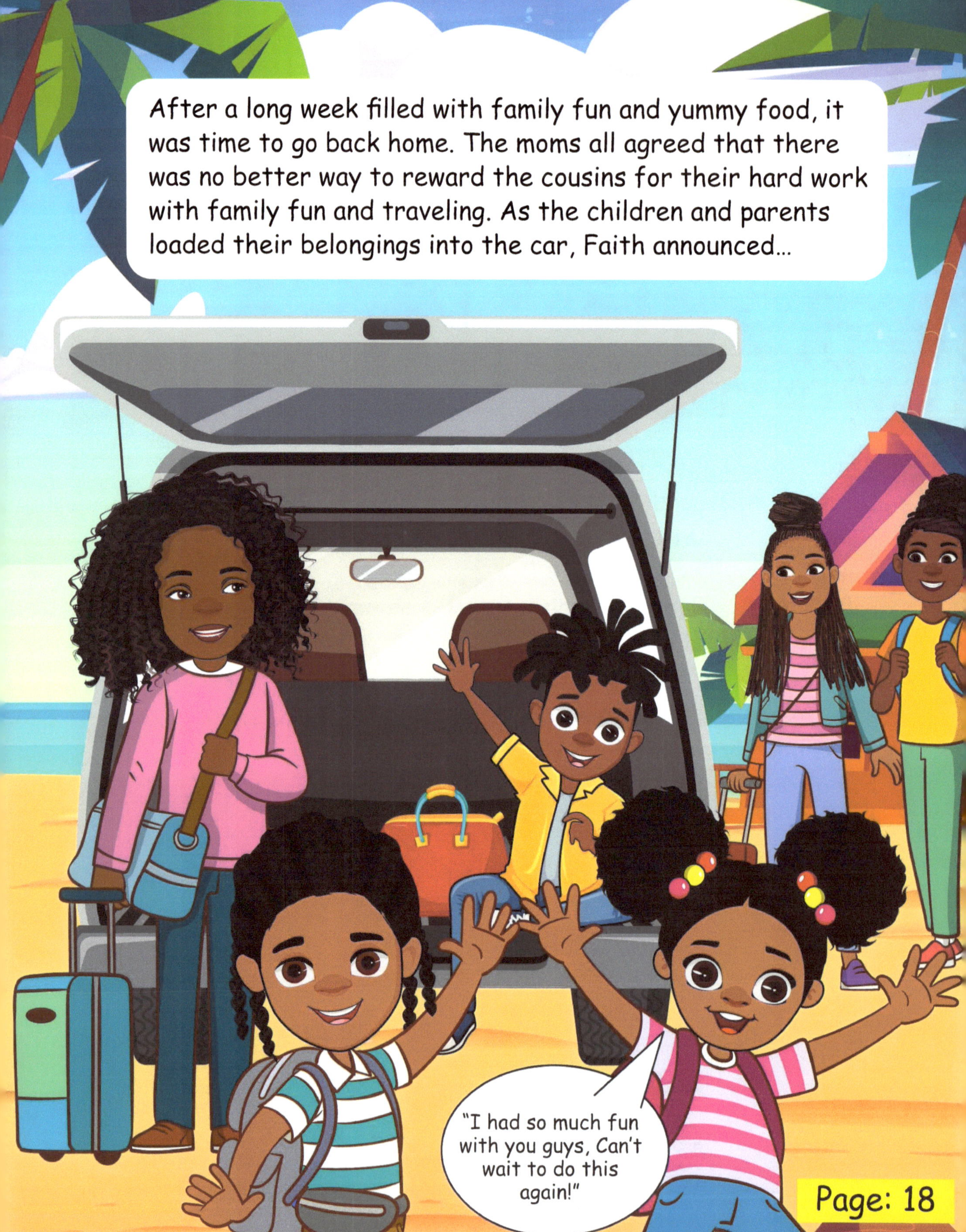
After a long week filled with family fun and yummy food, it was time to go back home. The moms all agreed that there was no better way to reward the cousins for their hard work with family fun and traveling. As the children and parents loaded their belongings into the car, Faith announced...
"I had so much fun with you guys, Can't wait to do this again!"

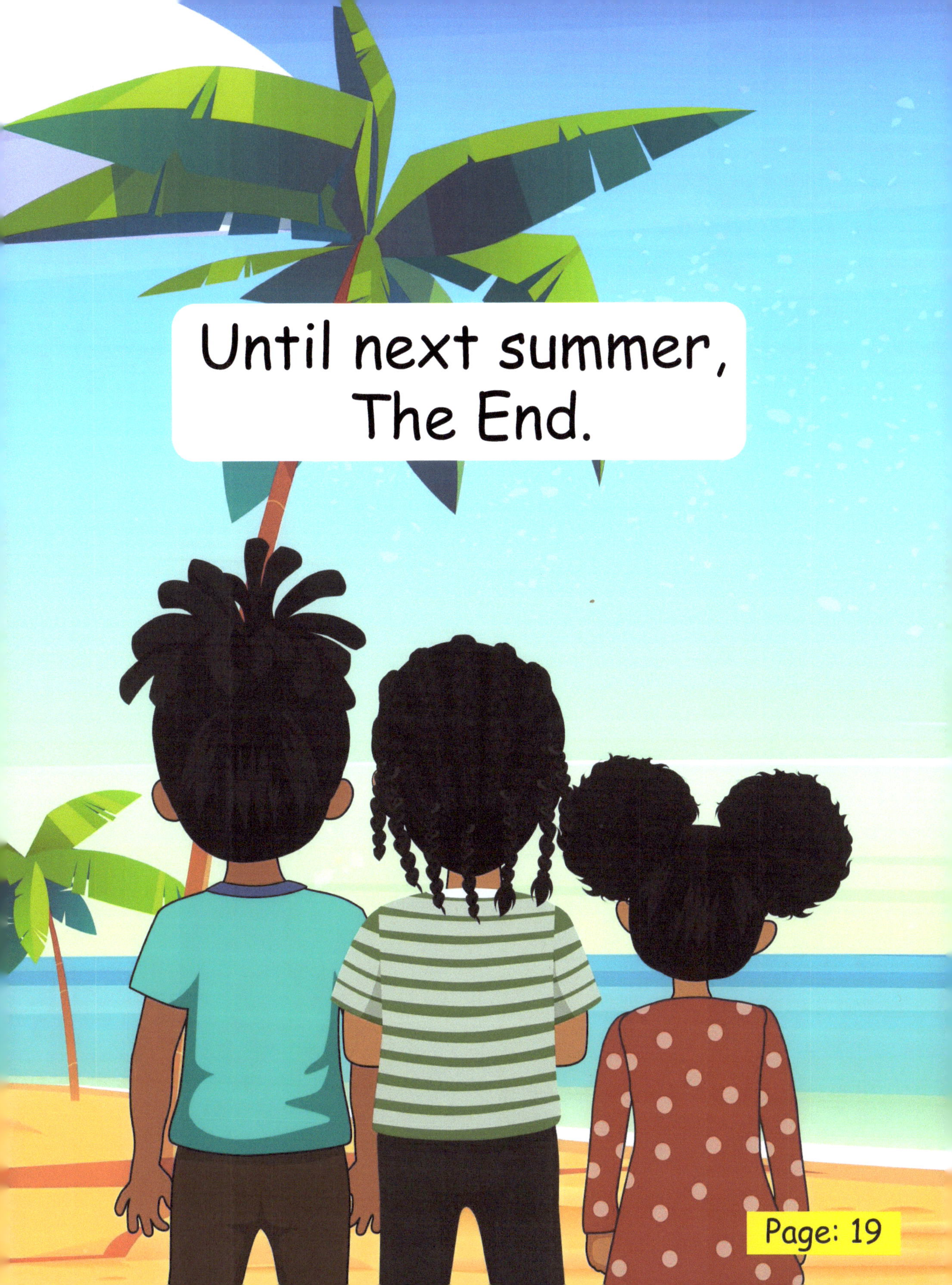
Until next summer,
The End.

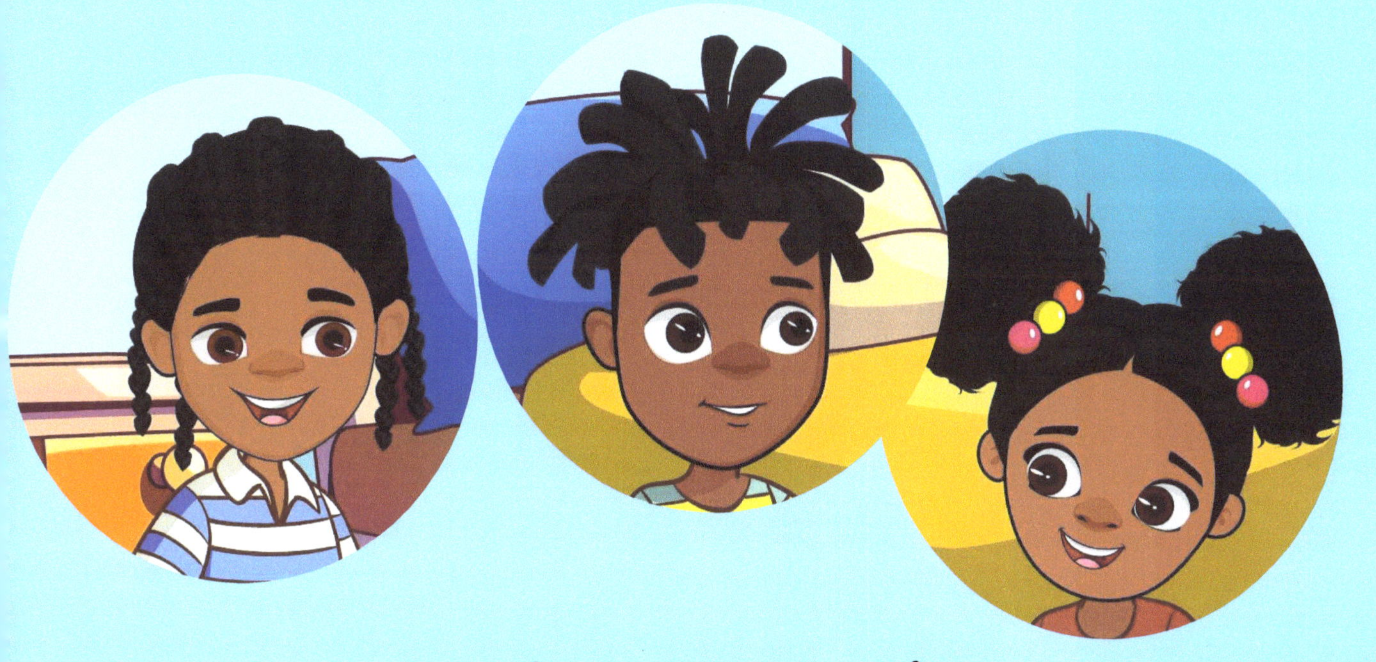

Sight Words Review

Let's practice some of the sight words from

A Day of Play

With LeVon, Langston, and Faith!

Summer Vacation

Pre-K Sight Words

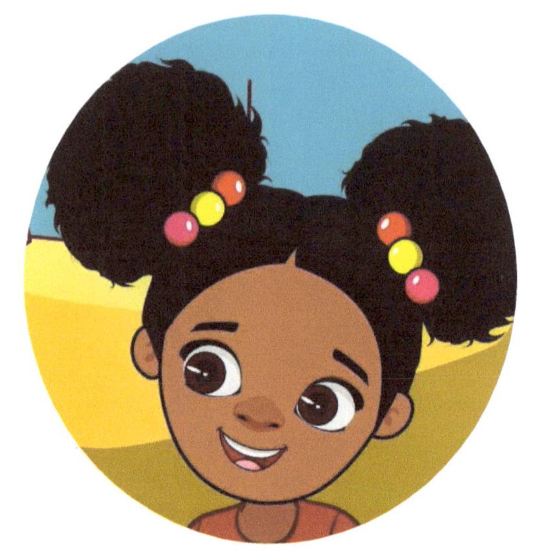

we	at	my	you
he	she	and	to
is	the	like	can
go	so	do	an
am	no	it	in
up	are	for	me

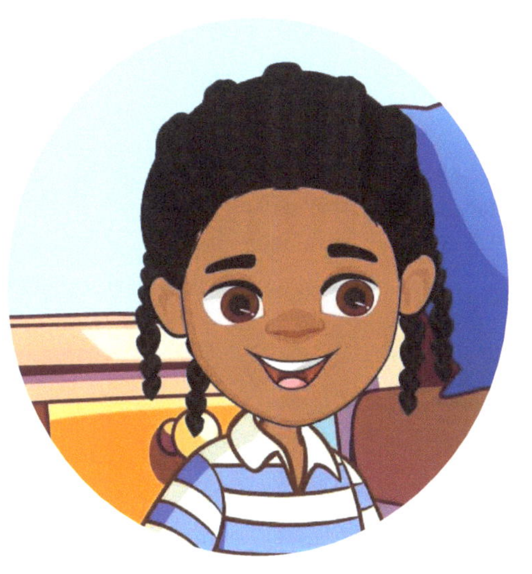

First Grade Sight Words

but	with	them	of
as	will	all	get
be	from	they	back
each	first	this	have
what	where	going	your
boy	girl	his	him
her	more	nake	write

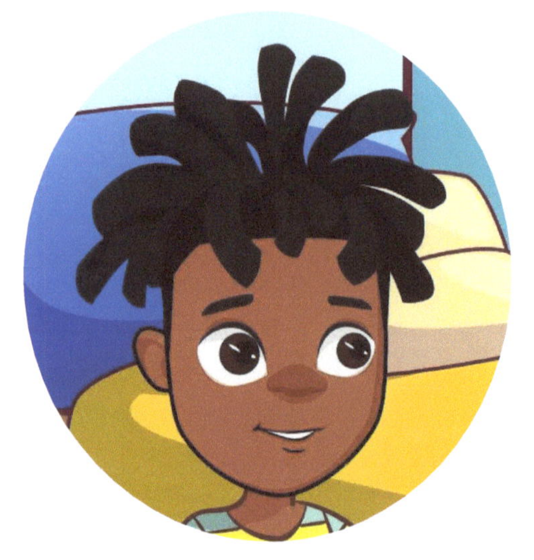

Second Grade Sight Words

into	our	both	almost
kind	most	old	their
give	any	sky	try
also	after	does	smal
think	good	today	change
year	move	new	place
under	able	again	air
behind	learn	work	great

www.ingramcontent.com/pod-product-compliance
Lightning Source LLC
LaVergne TN
LVHW070208110826
845147LV00002B/534

* 9 7 8 1 7 3 2 9 9 0 2 6 5 *